# The Third Sister Speaks

Anne Brontë–scenes from a life

Liliana A. Pasterska

Leaf by Leaf is an imprint of Cinnamon Press.
www.cinnamonpress.com

The right of Liliana A Pasterska to be identified as author of this work has been asserted by her in accordance with the Copyright, Designs and Patent Act, 1988. © 2021, Liliana A Pasterska.

ISBN 978-1-78864-938-4

British Library Cataloguing in Publication Data. A CIP record for this book can be obtained from the British Library.

All rights reserved. No part of this publication may be reproduced, stored in a retrieval system, or transmitted in any form or by any means, electronic, mechanical, photocopying, recording or otherwise without the prior written permission of the publishers. This book may not be lent, hired out, resold or otherwise disposed of by way of trade in any form of binding or cover other than that in which it is published, without the prior consent of the publishers.

Designed and typeset in Bodoni by Cinnamon Press. Cover design by Adam Craig from original artwork: James Elkington, Top Withens, iStock ID:1148290305.

Cinnamon Press is represented by Inpress Ltd.

Liliana A Pasterska was born in Poland and educated there as a paediatrician and psychiatrist. She worked in UK as a consultant psychiatrist for many years and became interested in the female condition, particularly in relation to the pioneering women writers of XIX century. Some of her poems have been published in the *Journal of the Gaskell Society* and in the anthologies of Manchester Stanza and Womanswrite groups. She is married with two adult children and lives in London.

## Acknowledgements

To Pamela Nash, the Artistic Director of Anne Brontë Bicentenary Celebration in Words and Music, who commissioned this writing. The event was supported by Arts Council England, the Ida Carroll Trust and the Hinrichsen Foundation. To Ann Dinsdale and Brontë Parsonage Museum. To writing associates in Womanswrite, Manchester Stanza and Elizabeth Gaskell House, in particular Theresa Sowerby, Almira Holmes and Philip Watts. Warm thank you to Jan Fortune and Adam Craig for the generosity of their encouragement and advice. Gratitude to my friends for their readings and never waning interest: Joanne Wilcox, Inga Wlosinska, Anna-Maria Gaj, Barbara Petecka, Penelope Hopwood, Christine Dean, Dorcas Kingham. My most special thanks to Jerzy, Dominika and Filip for their informed attentiveness and support.

# Contents

| | |
|---|---:|
| Introduction | 5 |
| Prologue: Reluctant Fugitive | 11 |
| Anne's Wish | 12 |
| Together | 14 |
| Walking with You | 15 |
| Writing | 16 |
| Growing Apart | 17 |
| Zenobia's Song | 18 |
| Divination | 19 |
| Anne's Book of Prayer | 20 |
| Moorland | 21 |
| The Third Sister Speaks | 22 |
| Agnes Grey—the governess | 23 |
| Dearest Branwell | 25 |
| Loosing You | 26 |
| Aunt Branwell | 27 |
| Stepping Out with Dr Who | 28 |
| York Minster | 29 |
| Handkerchief | 30 |
| Scarborough Sunset | 31 |
| Anniversary Visit | 32 |
| Epilogue: Anniversary Verse | 33 |

# Introduction

Liliana Pasterska is interested in Anne Brontë as a frontierswoman, a trailblazing writer of mid 19th century literature, who wrote on subjects considered unsuitable for a female writer and taboo in Victorian society. Consequently, she was harshly criticised by her contemporary reviewers and underestimated in comparison with her sisters. Anne wrote about gender inequality, marital abuse, the appalling position in which the female teachers often worked. The power of her observations and penetrating insights in depicting alcohol/substance abuse is also acute; perspicacious enough to be given to medical students of these conditions. Anne Brontë's poetry is equally telling in demonstrating her personal, spiritual and literary development from childhood to her untimely death at the age of 29.

The cycle of 'The Third Sister Speaks' was originally commissioned to fit a programme of music and words celebrating the writer's bicentenary at an event in Manchester.

for Nicolai, Teodora and Milosz

# The Third Sister Speaks
Anne Brontë–scenes from a life

# Prologue: Reluctant Fugitive

Reviewers, commentators!
In the midst of your pursuits I live
failed and failed again.
I am not surprised but oh! I do mind
with aching heart, stifled breath,
Oh! Do *fail better*! Past the critiques,
Mrs Gaskell, Charlotte's guard—

Am I such an enigma of a writer?
What I want for women,
female artists—is it so un-thinkable?
Do I have to wait? A century? Two?
The oppression, suppression, denials,
such marriages, work conditions—
not Gothic enough? Too real. Too true.

My poetry—is it the best kept secret?
The biography–in–waiting.
I bare my soul, my heart, my mind,
my nostalgia for innocence and trust.
Romantic provenance—a heritage
to leave behind, like childhood—
I leap into reality, the truth of it.

# Anne's Wish

*Age and experience I need, dear Papa*

                              (aged four)

and so we travel with you
here and there
gather things on our way
like this
pastel shaded pebbles
swirly shells    stones
we put them on a shelf
give to sister

distant lands    great battles
courtships    ladies    knights
we Google destinations    distances
Sir Walter's counties    Byronic borderlands—
Freedom Pass to Kings Cross    railcard to Leeds
Keighley taxi on narrow    wet lanes

child of the moorland
of wind and rain
reading and stories    buoyant faith
meet the children of society
face to face
the roads converge    link up
different belonging
only connect

destiny of women frustrates
bewildering ways of men incense
conspiring of society angers
you pine after life of your own
a gift of primroses
meeting on a country walk
flutter of the heart requited

romantic tales left behind
no *soft nonsense*
you stop at your *pillars of witness*
take your pen

# Together

there is no such thing as bad weather
for the two of us   wrapped up in layers
of years   twinned—we knot our memories
softly   like scarves   my hand in yours

words come like sunrays   wind   rain
we string them along empty pages
we see what we could not see before
a country new   without loneliness   woe

beyond East   further than West
past melting fires of the Earth's hub   we travelled
the gardens kept all scents of then
trees   on their roots forever young

now sing of different silence—
to remember what was not forgotten
to find what was never lost
we travelled so

# Walking with You

your dress    shawl    heathery yarns
skirts in the blow    strong boots
the way we walk    follow each other—
this space can take it    take us

we step in open arms of moor
narrow    stony path shines wet
yesterday's wintry downpour soft
on soil    splattering water    mud

rivulets trickle    chattering
down the slopes    pool in holes
rest    full of clouds    sky—
waves of heather move to and fro

in sharp northerly    glow chocolatey
brown in today's spring sunshine
sparkling flowerets of last summer
bleaching in heathland's air

blue-on-blue    starry—
I look at the spray    now on our table
spiky leaves already capped green
tiny azure clusters holding fast

# Writing

Tea finished—it is that time of day—
we close the dining room door,
still the evening sounds of the house,
you go to stoke the fire,
I watch the sky's weather-prophecies,
the flight of peregrine in the wild.

It is the time of stories.
Small books on the table, waiting.
We return to our lands of old
as if they needed to grow up as well,
needed our blood, breath, rhythm of hand,
ready for coming off age with us.

Shoulder to shoulder we circle the room,
our bodies back on the moorland—
as if made of the moors' sound, scent,
movement—in the tranquillity of room
what is this rush of joy, excitement
of mind, the pull of yet unwritten page—

## Growing Apart

sunlight shadows
dry stone patterns
purple swarms of heather
scramble up the slope    sway
their murmuring tunes

open moors fill the horizon—
in the cloister of valley
where the sycamore tree
stands guard at a farmhouse
—song of a blackbird

startled grouse bursts out—
a flurry of flapping wings
bees interrupted    you extend
your hand protectively
I do not reach out mine

not anymore    I have outgrown
our twinning    silently
you hardly take notice
when we step out together
you still take us to

misty shores of distant lands—
waves flow    surging into rhymes
the smooth driftwood of minds
we sail the sea of moorland

# Zenobia's Song

in Gondal time    summers are long
days meander like tales—
I met a young boy walking up the path
vast and deep like the seas were his eyes

all around us the gardens    the jasmines in bloom
stood still    even jay had stopped singing
when he looked and we knew this love from before
but he turned and along winding path was leaving

and now when my whole life has been much too short
to walk all the roads    all the paths of searching
he now comes back to me    the man of ancient eyes—
bringing all the world's flowers    sweetly scented

# Divination

will there be no walk again tomorrow—
feet warmed at the fire fender
I stop my rocking chair toing-and-froing
leave my sisters writing    walk into garden

the hawthorn branches hang winter-bare
heavy with water    drops gather themselves
for a perfect fall    catch the setting sunlight
this way and that

cloudless sky    blush on solid silver
returns my questioning gaze—
writings of great designs    I stand in awe
star among stars

how blind I have been    accept and wait
paradise deferred    all I believed there was
I return to my desk    my notes
against ill times    against death—my weapon

# Anne's Book of Prayer

small rectangle of a book
winey red cover   tooled with gold
familiar day-to-day keeper
of invocations   bonds

shall I open it like a window
on a new Spring day
keep it ajar   for life's breath

follow with my voice
songs from the different land
soothing for the troubles

live in its home
with my burnt offerings
burnt hopes

# Moorland

is there a map
in the mind of God
for the changes of light
on the moorland?

tangle of tracks
aiming at the sky
the taste of heather
on my breath

grassland winds
carry my thoughts
beyond the hills
over the horizon

Is there a map
in the mind of God
for the darkness and
light   my only load?

# The Third Sister Speaks (a found poem)

*Preface to second Edition: Tennant of Wildfell Hall*

I am a teller of truth   a seer—can you hear me?
I am not saying what I do simply to amuse    I worry
worry about girls    the state of their education—
no preparation for life    nothing but dinner party polish

truth always has its own moral
a kernel of it   inside every nut of a story
a jewel at the bottom of a well    if dared to plunge into
will you receive it    scorn it?

dealing with vice    is it better to cover it
with flowers    or to depict it as it is
reveal the snares    pitfalls    alive in any respectable society
or to conceal the facts    with delicacy

this whispering *peace    peace* where there is none
leaves the young to wring their knowledge of life
from the misery of their own experience
the doors of elegant houses    family rooms

women's bedrooms    all firmly shut    the happy ever after—
I would love to write for innocent pleasure!
but is it not a writer's duty to speak up    to disguise not—
society's mores    its taboos    unpalatable truth

I write    carefully    from life    not to gratify my own taste
not to ingratiate myself with readers    I wish to benefit them
I observe without being noticed    still the rebellious beat
of my heart    still myself    I write    I want to be useful

I tell life stories
will you look    with me    for the kernel of truth?

## Agnes Grey—the governess

1

And so
I have my way!

trunks must be packed
drawers emptied    books taken down

our last ramble on the moor
walk around garden   house
we together feed Keeper   Flossy
I play the last tune on our old piano
sing my song for papa.

I am departing early
hasty breakfast
fond embraces    a kiss
for the cat

hired gig descends the hill
crosses the valley—
I look back
the village spire
old Parsonage
in a slanting beam of sunshine
I turn again    face the road

a governess!
to be a governess—
children    tender plants
minds    unfolding day by day
I go out into the world
I can work

2

children—

my work bag into fire
my desk out of the window
snatched back only just
tumult in the garden
bootless     hatless in the snow—

what was it I said?
tender plants? unfolding minds?
to be fair
they said to me
they would be naughty
with a glee

I am not willing to give it up
neither a servant nor a family friend
feeling like a thistle seed
born on the wind
I must stand alone


3

snow is lying thickly on the ground
sun's shadowing its folds in blue
despite the weather my former charges are
coming before their weddings     last *rendez-vous*
they think so differently now
know to marry head and heart
in the resonance of our bonds
friendship has sneaked in     to last

# Dearest Branwell

brother Icarus
I wish   I had wings
to fly you up    back
into un-troubled sky

mother-of-the-moors
have mercy
I give you to her
to hold against
cursed bedtimes

your hidden knife
no help
room on fire
your body
candle sweating out

I saw you
through father's tears
felt your hand over mine
skeletal    my hand in yours
as you rise    embrace    part
my unready heart

# Loosing You

just awake
but the dark invader
is already there
night-long
behind the eyes
caged in against ribs
heavy in muscles

the sun
disconnects—
intoxicates birds
glimmers silver on the leaves
spotlights the dark heart
a cloudy day never could—
garden of gifts too far

turn away
from the window
move slowly    smile
in the rhythm
of your steps
grey passage of days
know your way

# Aunt Branwell

In her sisterly visit from Cornwall,
across the sea, miles of open country,
fate plays its hand—she stays:
six motherless children, bereft father,
reduced circumstances—she takes over,
dependable like her ardent faith.

Pieties commune, schooling buzz heartens,
after work well done, gaieties can be had,
shanties, ballads, stories—from Land End's
piskies to the bog country's leprechauns,
Cornish burr, Irish lilt—pair of pattens
clicking, patting, on droughty stone floors—
her homely rhythms.

Twenty years later she ponders
strange familiarity of this foreign land,
wuthering climate, poor, hard working
people, children—now young adults...
Village chimneys spewing smoke,
surrounding moors nothing like her sea,
not a lugger, not a sail in sight.

Anne, dearest Anne—adrenaline rushes—
then sharing her room, bed, time,
toddling at her skirts, hand reaching out—
now an indomitable spirit, burning quietly,
holding patiently to her judgements.
Devoted to her dead mother,
to her aunt never less than own child.

# Stepping Out with Dr Who

Mother's smelling salt bottle    summery trinket
timeless painted flowers framed with gilt heart
against life's brevity    illness    death
from mother to daughter    and daughter again

Penzance to Yorkshire the North Devon way
storms    rocks that shatter    strand
survivor of the shipwreck and the deep
across the sea    message of resilience

*this?* Time Lord quizzes
*your mother's smelling salts?*

he points the direction    otherworldly rogue
offers his arm    and I    dear Reader    take it
and we go there    Streptomycin's age
white powder    ending bacillus' carnage
so we can be    so I can be
can work    take stand—

so much to write    who will I be    what life—

we sweep the moors in time-travelling steps
he listens    wind tuning    heather singing—
we whirl    we swirl    we spin
over brook    across generations—
breathing so light    heart so glad
could it be dancing—

# York Minster

the whole city is moving with us
congregation of town dwellings
crowds along the street
until we arrive    houses part
open their tree-fingered arms
and you are there    out of the sky
Minster *in a vesture of gold*
light streams down the façade
down the towers    the sentinels—
past and future meets here
columns    finials    pinnacles
running high    upwards    higher
                                       soaring

Inside
they stop my nursing chair
the nave fills with light
floating dapple of gold    ruby red
throngs through the traceries—
my eyes on the nave's parade
to the crystalline light of the East
is this the Angel's voice
of seventh might
land-and-sea spanning
murmur of seven thunders
sigh of secrets under seven sills—
the beginning and the end
the dawning and vanishing—
my sense of revelation

*If finite power can do this...*

# Handkerchief

We walk through the house in her footsteps,
through the setting of greatness that thrills,
we marvel at the smallness of things—beds,
shoes, a pretty bonnet, gloves, a dress,
her mind, belying its embodiment, transcends
the physicality of build, age, strength—

When a handkerchief comes into view, thoughts arrest—
large cotton square, finely patterned, stained
with blood, in faded markings of its own.
It shocks—faded no longer, glowing bright,
speaking its tale of sorrow, courage, loss,
a fate of untimeliness.

# Scarborough Sunset

in my window chair I know
it's time to turn the other way
to the sea     the sky rising from waters
dressing for the night

this morning I still had a walk
on the beach     I left in sand
my footprints     light     final
had to be helped back to my room

path edged with laburnum
scented with lilacs—
I leave behind Spring's exuberance—
dandelion coffee     a sip

was I ever anything but a candle
burning away into silence—
crumpled folds of sorrow
a discarded dress on the floor

I step off my narrow way into colour
into moonlight     starlight—
this sunset     awash with sea
is this my sun coming up

## Anniversary Visit

through the trees
we first see the church   its walls
the colour of seashore sand—
sea-breeze sighs in leaves
sun adjusts its canvas

we walk round   cross the little
passage to smaller cemetery
your weathered headstone—
a bunch of roadside flowers there
offering of a seashell     a pebble

I can glimpse from here the sight of sea
it takes on all the shades of moorlands

# Epilogue: Anniversary Verse

life story starts    life story ends
short    circumscribed    observant—
different calendars being then
for house towering over graves
the village on its slope below
heaving with industry    bad water

writing of secrecy    urge    revolt
moorlands' summons of release
truth-saying for elucidation
against protesting generation
making new before *Make it new!*
became the 'it' call of the era

sneaking taste for the modern—
pages of neat script erupting
in living rooms    nurseries    bedrooms
in sleepy residences    removed
from new scenery flaring up
machines    factories    trains—

with no room of my own
no money
here is my fiction truer than truth
poetry—*my way*

www.ingramcontent.com/pod-product-compliance
Ingram Content Group UK Ltd.
Pitfield, Milton Keynes, MK11 3LW, UK
UKHW042146020225
454580UK00005B/131